USING SCALES AND BALANCES

Lorijo Metz

PowerKiDS press

New York

To Valentine, may your mind and heart always be balanced

Published in 2013 by The Rosen Publishing Group, Inc.
29 East 21st Street, New York, NY 10010

First Edition

Editor: Amelie von Zumbusch
Book Design: Kate Laczynski

Photo Credits: Cover © iStockphoto.com/Les Howard; pp. 4–5 © iStockphoto.com/xefstock; p. 6 Mandy Godbehear/
Shutterstock.com; p. 7 Felix Mizioznikov/Shutterstock.com; p. 8 iStockphoto/Thinkstock; p. 9 (top) Zoonar/Thinkstock;
p. 9 (bottom) auremar/Shutterstock.com; p. 10 Take 2 Productions/Brand X Pictures/Getty Images; p. 11 oksana2010/
Shutterstock.com; p. 12 Charles D. Winters/Photo Researchers/Getty Images; p. 13 AVAVA/Shutterstock.com; p. 14 (top) No
Hendrickson/Digital Vision/Getty Images; p. 14 (bottom) Jack Hollingsworth/Photodisc/Getty Images; p. 15 GIPhotoStock/
Photo Researchers/Getty Images; p. 16 Southern Illinois University/Photo Researchers/Getty Images; p. 17 corepics/
Shutterstock.com; p. 19 Michael Blann/Lifesize/Getty Images; p. 20 Shanta Giddens/Shutterstock.com; p. 21 Matt Meadow
Peter Arnold/Getty Images; p. 22 Coprid/Shutterstock.com.

Library of Congress Cataloging-in-Publication Data

Metz, Lorijo.
 Using scales and balances / by Lorijo Metz. — 1st ed.
    p. cm. — (Science tools)
 Includes index.
 ISBN 978-1-4488-9686-8 (library binding) — ISBN 978-1-4488-9830-5 (pbk.) —
 ISBN 978-1-4488-9831-2 (6-pack)
 1. Balances (Weighing instruments)—Juvenile literature. 2. Rulers (Instruments)—Juvenile literature. I. Title.
 QC107.M48 2013
 681'.2—dc23
                        2012029968

Manufactured in the United States of America

CPSIA Compliance Information: Batch #W13PK4: For Further Information contact Rosen Publishing, New York, New York at 1-800-237-9932

CONTENTS

What Are Scales and Balances?

If you have ever played on a seesaw, you know how a balance works! Suppose two friends sit on either end of a seesaw, at equal distances from the center. When they lift up their legs, the side the heavier person is sitting on goes down. If both friends weigh the same, the seesaw remains balanced. Balances are tools for comparing how much things weigh. A scale is another tool used to weigh things.

It might surprise you how often people weigh things. Doctors weigh their patients. People weigh foods they buy in stores. Weighing things is a part of many science **experiments**.

These kids are working with a balance. Have you ever used one?

Mass, Weight, and Gravity

Everything, including you, is made of **matter**. Matter is made of tiny parts called atoms. **Mass** is a measure of how much matter something has.

Weight depends on **gravity**. Gravity is a force, or pull, between objects with mass. Weight is a measure of that pull. The more mass something has, the stronger its pull.

Any ball you kick up will eventually fall back to Earth. This happens because of Earth's gravity.

Your weight depends on gravity, but your mass does not.

Because Earth is so huge, its gravity is strong enough to keep people and other things from floating off into space. You weigh more on Earth than you would on the Moon because Earth has more mass. However, your mass remains the same no matter where you are.

Measuring Mass

In the United States, we use the US customary system. We measure mass in ounces and pounds. A pound equals 16 ounces. For objects with more mass, like elephants, we use tons. There are 2,000 pounds in 1 ton.

Other countries use the metric system. Scientists use it, too. It measures mass in grams and kilograms.

BATHROOM SCALE

Weight in pounds

Weight in kilograms

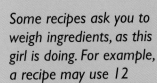
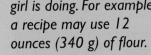

● **Weight in kilograms**

● **Weight in pounds**

Some recipes ask you to weigh ingredients, as this girl is doing. For example, a recipe may use 12 ounces (340 g) of flour.

There are 1,000 grams in a kilogram. For heavier objects, the metric system uses tonnes. There are 1,000 kilograms in 1 tonne. Scientists use nanograms to measure things that are so small you can't see them. They need special computers to weigh them.

How to Use a Balance

Balances work by comparing the mass of two or more objects. They have three main parts, much like a seesaw. A beam, or long arm, balances on a **fulcrum**, or center point. A pan hangs from each end of the beam. To use a balance, put the object you want to weigh in one pan. Place standard weights, or objects whose weight is already known, in the other pan until the scale is balanced.

The gold-colored objects this student is putting on the scale are standard weights.

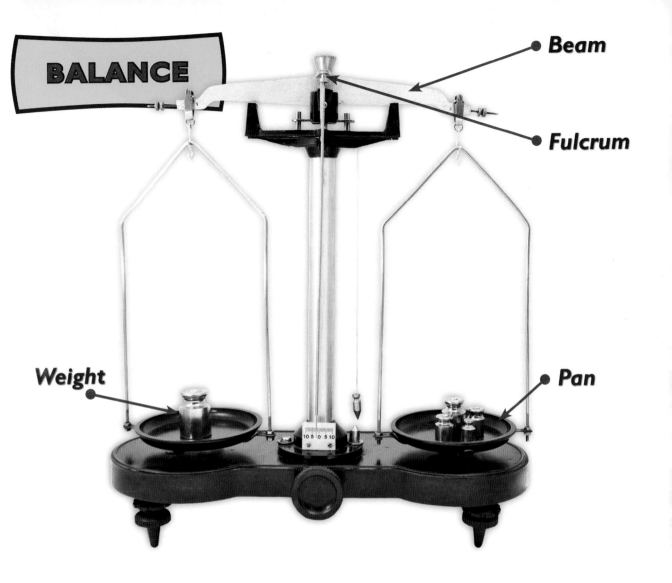

BALANCE

Beam

Fulcrum

Weight

Pan

To measure 6 ounces (170 g) of candy, place standard weights measuring 6 ounces (170 g) on one pan. Then add candy to the other pan until the two pans hang evenly.

11

How to Use a Triple Beam Balance

A triple beam balance has three weighted beams. The beams measure in 100-gram, 10-gram, and .1-gram **increments**. There is a pan on one side of the balance. On the other side, there are a pointer and an arrow.

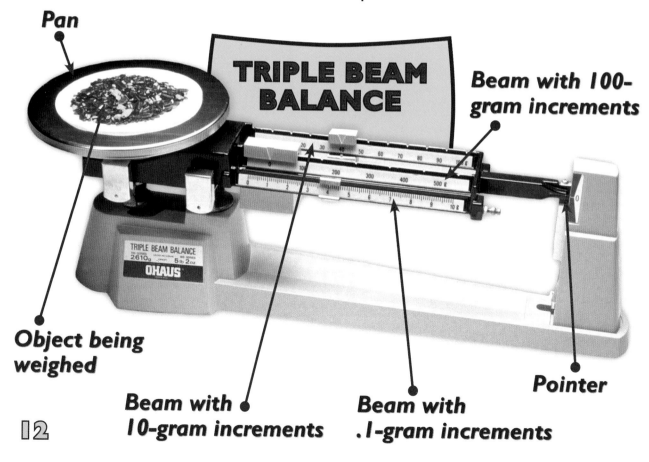

Pan

Beam with 100-gram increments

Object being weighed

Beam with 10-gram increments

Beam with .1-gram increments

Pointer

To use the balance, slide all the weights to their zero setting. The pointer should line up with the arrow. If not, there should be a knob near the pan for adjustments. Next, place the object you are weighing on the pan. Move the weights across the beams until the arrow is pointing straight again. Add the measurements together to get the total mass.

A balance beam scale works much the same way a triple beam scale does. Weights on different beams measure different increments.

Spring Scales

The English scientist Robert Hooke discovered he could weigh objects by hanging them from metal springs and measuring how much the springs stretched. He could also measure weight by how much the object **compressed**, or pushed down, a spring.

The pan of a spring scale can be either above (left) or below (right) the scale's spring and dial.

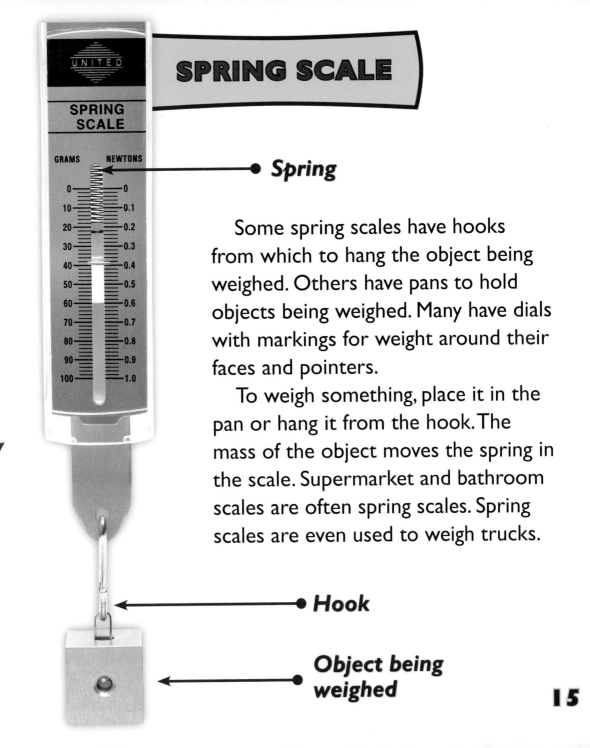

SPRING SCALE

United

SPRING SCALE

GRAMS   NEWTONS

0	0
10	0.1
20	0.2
30	0.3
40	0.4
50	0.5
60	0.6
70	0.7
80	0.8
90	0.9
100	1.0

● *Spring*

Some spring scales have hooks from which to hang the object being weighed. Others have pans to hold objects being weighed. Many have dials with markings for weight around their faces and pointers.

To weigh something, place it in the pan or hang it from the hook. The mass of the object moves the spring in the scale. Supermarket and bathroom scales are often spring scales. Spring scales are even used to weigh trucks.

● *Hook*

Object being weighed

Digital Scales

There are many times when knowing the exact weight of something is more than just interesting, it is important. When creating life-saving drugs or running experiments, scientists depend on exact weight measurements.

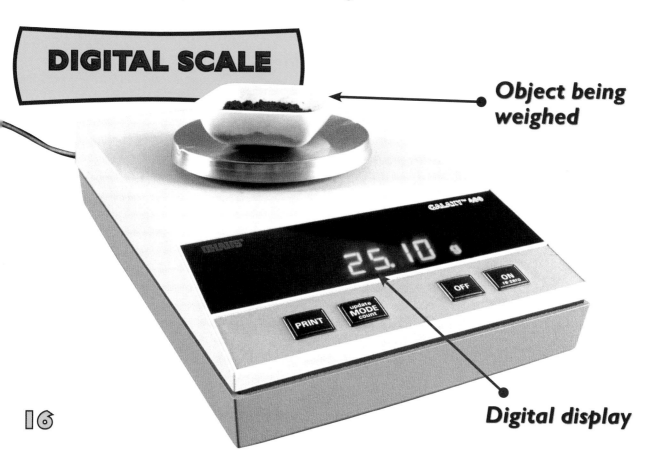

DIGITAL SCALE

Object being weighed

Digital display

Digital scales give more exact measurements than spring scales. Inside a digital scale is a load cell. A load cell has an **electric current** running through it. Objects placed on a digital scale bend the load cell inside, changing the current and sending a message to a tiny computer chip, called a microchip. The microchip runs the digital display that shows you the weight.

17

Planning an Experiment

When scientists want to test a **hypothesis**, or idea about how something works, they create experiments. Tools, such as scales or balances, must work the same way each time a scientist conducts an experiment. Balances should be cleaned and scales zeroed out. To zero out a scale, make sure the digital display or the pointer is at zero.

What if your experiment involves a liquid? To weigh liquids, you must place them in something, such as a cup. To get only the weight of the liquid but not the cup, zero out the scale with the empty cup on it. Then, add the liquid to the cup.

Scientists use scales and balances to measure all sorts of things, from chemicals to chickens.

Understanding Density

Once you figure out the mass and volume of objects, you can compare their density.

You cannot always tell how much something weighs by looking at it. Fill one cup with water and another cup the same size with cooking oil. The water and the oil both have the same **volume**, or take up the same amount of space. If you weigh the two cups on a scale or balance, though, you will find that the cup with water weighs more.

While mass is how much matter something has, **density** is how tightly packed together that matter is. Water takes up the same amount of space as oil, but it has more matter. Denser objects weigh more than less dense objects of the same size.

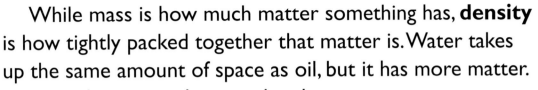

The red balls on the right have a smaller volume than the yellow balls on the left but weigh the same. This means the red balls must be denser than the yellow ones.

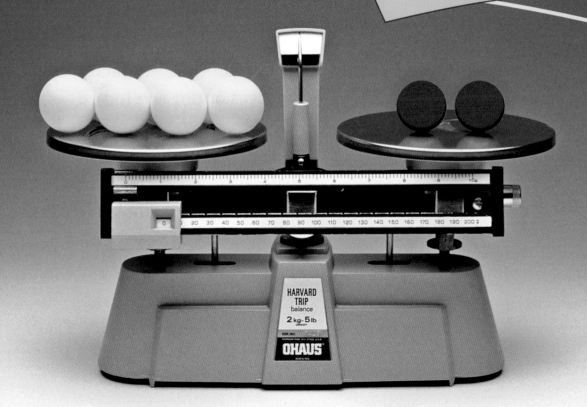

Using a balance or scale, compare the densities of different foods found in your kitchen. You will need:

1. One balance or small scale
2. Five small cups, all of the same size and weight
3. Five foods from your kitchen, such as milk, flour, salt, vegetable oil, and raisins

Fill each cup with one food. In a notebook, list each food. Without lifting the cups, make guesses about the foods' weights. Which one will weigh the most? Which one will be the lightest? Write your guess beside each food. Using a balance or a scale, compare the foods' weights. Did you guess correctly? Was something heavier or lighter than you thought it would be? Why do you think that was?

GLOSSARY

compressed (kum-PREST) Squeezed something into a smaller place.

density (DEN-seh-tee) The heaviness of an object compared to its size.

digital (DIH-juh-tul) Having a display that uses numbers.

electric current (ih-LEK-trik KUR-ent) A flow of electricity.

experiments (ik-SPER-uh-ments) Actions or steps taken to learn more about something.

fulcrum (FUL-krum) The point on which something turns.

gravity (GRA-vih-tee) The force that causes objects to move toward each other. The bigger an object is, the more gravity it has.

hypothesis (hy-PAH-theh-ses) A possible answer to a problem.

increments (ING-kreh-ments) Amounts by which things are spaced out.

mass (MAS) The amount of matter in something.

matter (MA-ter) Anything that has weight and takes up space.

volume (VOL-yoom) The amount of space that matter takes up.

INDEX

WEBSITES

Due to the changing nature of Internet links, PowerKids Press has developed an online list of websites related to the subject of this book. This site is updated regularly. Please use this link to access the list:

www.powerkidslinks.com/scto/scale/